8/90

FOREWORD

"Frontiers of America" dramatizes some of the explorations and discoveries of real pioneers in simple, uncluttered text. America's spirit of adventure is seen in these early people who faced dangers and hardship blazing trails, pioneering new water routes, becoming Western heroes as well as legends, and building log forts and houses as they settled in the wilderness.

Although today's explorers and adventurers face different frontiers, the drive and spirit of these early pioneers in America's past still serve as an inspiration.

ABOUT THE AUTHOR

During her years as a teacher and reading consultant in elementary schools, Mrs. McCall developed a strong interest in the people whose pioneering spirit built our nation. When she turned to writing as a full-time occupation, this interest was the basis for much of her work. She is the author of many books and articles for children and adults, and co-author of elementary school social studies textbooks.

Frontiers of America

PIONEERING
on the
PLAINS

By Edith McCall

Illustrations by Carol Rogers

ᗁ CHILDRENS PRESS ™

CHICAGO

Library of Congress Cataloging in
Publication Data
McCall, Edith S
    Pioneering on the Plains.
    1.   Garland, Hamlin, 1860-1940—Juvenile
fiction.   2.   Ruede, Howard, 1854-1925—
Juvenile fiction.   I.   Title
PZ7.M1229.Pf   62-15638
ISBN 0-516-03358-1

New 1980 Edition
Copyright© 1962 by Regensteiner
Publishing Enterprises, Inc.
All rights reserved. Published
simultaneously in Canada.
Printed in the United States of America.
4 5 6 7 8 9 10 11 R 93 92 91 90 89 88

CONTENTS

Moving Day

To young Hamlin Garland, home had always been the little frame house in the lovely green valley in western Wisconsin. His world reached a little way into the woods behind the house, but not far, for in the dark woods lived bobcats and wolves. A boy might meet even a bear or an Indian.

At the bottom of the valley, below the house, ran a brown road, dusty in summer and frozen into sharp-edged ruts in winter. Hamlin's world went as far up this road as the curve where it left the valley and as far down as the village where Grandfather Garland lived. But his world never went as far as the wonderful city of La Crosse, twelve miles away, where the Mississippi River steamboats hooted hoarsely of their comings and goings.

Then, one fall day when Hamlin was eight years old, his father said, "I've sold the farm. We'll move to the west."

Still it did not seem real that the Garland family could be leaving the valley, until the cold day in

February when the old wooden clock was taken down from the kitchen shelf where it had ticked away each day of Hamlin's life. He watched as his mother wrapped it in towels and laid it in a packing box.

Outside, there was a jingling of bells as Mr. Garland pulled Doll and Queen to a stop. The old farm wagon, made into a sleigh for the winter, stood just outside the door. Mr. Garland unhitched the team and took the horses back to the barn to be in out of the cold while the sleigh was being loaded. He was back in a few minutes.

"Is everything ready to go, Belle?" he asked. His eyes were bright and his voice was tight with excitement.

Mrs. Garland was taking down the picture of General Grant from the place where it had hung since Mr. Garland came home from the War Between the States three years earlier. Hamlin saw the bare place left on the wall where the picture had hung. In that moment, he felt suddenly homeless. He knew his mother felt it, too, as she handed the picture to Hamlin.

"Wrap it in that quilt, Hamlin. The chairs and chests are ready, Richard. Come, Harriet and Frank.

Help me pack the dishes."

Ten-year-old Harriet and six-year-old Frank helped take dishes from the shelves and pack them carefully into a box of clothing and bedding. Into this box, too, went the two special treasures from the clock shelf. One was a shell which Mr. Garland had brought from a journey to the Gulf of Mexico. The other was his soldier's medal for bravery, which Hamlin thought meant his father was the greatest man in the world. Its leather case was almost worn out from Hamlin's handling it so much.

"It will be yours someday, when you are a man," his father had told him.

Now Hamlin helped his father take the chairs out to the sleigh. The room was growing chilly, for the fire in the stove had been left to die down. With the door open, the winter cold swept inside.

"Now the table, Hamlin," Mr. Garland said.

When the table was gone, only the stove was left. Hamlin came back into the house and closed the door to shut out the wind. It was strange to see the empty room, already looking as if no family loved it. Things he had never noticed before glared at him now, as if in anger at having their coverings stripped away. There was the dark stain on the windowsill where a potted geranium had always been, the crack in an upper pane of glass, and the pathway across the floor, worn bare of varnish.

Mr. Garland wasted no time in looking about. He was taking the stove pipe apart, and the black soot fell to the floor as he pulled the pipe loose from the ceiling.

"We'll put these pipes on the load after the stove is in the sleigh," he said. "I'll need your help again in a moment, Hamlin."

Hamlin took one last look at his "nesting place" under the stove. The stove was a grand thing, with swelled-out, polished iron sides above high-stepping legs. The oven was on the top, so there was plenty of room underneath for a boy to curl up on the floor. Hamlin had spent many hours there, studying the pictures of fat hogs and wavy-haired cattle in the *Farmer's Annual* after he had read every printed word in the house, or sometimes just dreaming of adventures in far-off Arabia.

The stove's warm sides felt good to Hamlin's hands as he helped his father ease it out to the sleigh. Now the house was empty. Ropes were tied around the load. Doll and Queen were brought back from the barn and backed into place to pull the sleigh. The little herd of milk cows was brought from the barn, too, following after Old Spot, whose halter rope was tied to the back of the sleigh. Behind the cows came flea-bitten old Josh, pulling the one-seater in which Mrs. Garland, Harriet and Frank were to ride.

Hamlin and his father climbed onto the seat of the sleigh. Without a backward look at the house, Mr. Garland cried out in a ringing voice, "Forward, march!" and flipped the reins.

With a great pull and much slipping of hoofs in the icy dooryard, Doll and Queen started the sleigh moving forward. The cows bellowed and followed after Old Spot, who had no choice but to walk along behind the sleigh. Last of all, Josh, with a great sigh, leaned into his harness. The little parade was on its way, and the Garlands looked no more on their home in the lovely Wisconsin valley.

Two hours later they saw the city of La Crosse spread out before them. It lay cupped in the low hills that edged the Mississippi River. It was a place of wonder to the children. Hamlin stood up in the sleigh, trying to see more.

"You should see it in summer, Hamlin," Mr. Garland said. "It is quiet now, for the lumbermen are almost all up in the woods cutting more pine trees for the mills you see over there at the edge of town. In summer, the town is full, and the steamboats are lined up at the river front."

The road led right into the frozen ruts of the main street, and from there to the edge of the Mississippi River. There could be no steamboats now, for the river was almost frozen over. Great sheets of ice reached out from each shore, but they did not meet in the middle. A black, angry serpent of water kept them apart.

No bridge had been built over the river. In the summer, a ferryboat took people, their horses and their wagons across to Minnesota or back again. Now that so much of the river was frozen, a small wooden bridge had been set onto the ice, crossing over the ugly dark water.

Mrs. Garland looked at the flimsy bridge. "Richard, will it hold under our heavy load?" she asked.

Dick Garland had stopped his team and walked back to see that all was well. His eyes were sparkling. Just ahead was Minnesota, stepping-stone to the land of his dreams — Iowa, where the prairies stretched for miles and miles, just waiting for a pioneer's plow.

He laughed at his wife's fears. "Of course it will hold, Belle. Let's be on our way."

Hamlin was out of the sleigh, too. His father spoke to him on the way back to the waiting team.

"You will have to walk across the river, Hamlin. The cows may give us a little trouble. You get them started on the bridge."

Hamlin took his eyes from that rickety bridge that waved in the sweep of the wind down the river. It was made of just a few planks and poles nailed together, with a single handrail on one side. Hamlin was more frightened than his mother, but he couldn't say so. His father expected him to be a "man" at all times.

"Yes, sir," was all he said.

Mr. Garland, always the soldier, called out again, "Forward, march!" With a slipping and sliding of hoofs, the horses began their trip across the ice.

"Moo-OO-oo!" bellowed Old Spot. And "Moo-OO-oo-oo!" complained all her followers.

Josh whinnied and stood still after the first time he slipped on the ice.

"Richard!" called Mrs. Garland above the bellowing of the cows.

Dick Garland looked back for just a moment. "We'll come back for you! Stay there!" he yelled.

He could not look back for long, for Doll and Queen were stepping onto the little swaying bridge. The end of the bridge reached only about three feet onto the ice.

"Easy there!" called Mr. Garland, and pulled the reins a little to the left. One slip of hoofs on the icy planks and the whole loaded sleigh could go into the Mississippi.

One step at a time, Doll and Queen moved forward, seeming to sense the danger. Even so, the bridge swayed up and down with each movement of the big hoofs. Hamlin, watching, felt his heart turn as icy as the river as he thought of walking above and so near that black swirl of water.

It was time for Old Spot to step onto the bridge. For a moment she held back, letting the halter rope stretch out full length. Hamlin slapped her on the flanks.

"Get along there!" he said, making himself sound much braver than he felt.

Old Spot moved forward. All Hamlin's attention went to getting the other cows to follow her, one at a time, onto the swaying bridge. By now, the bridge boards were making cracking sounds from all the weight on them. When the last cow stepped onto the bridge, Hamlin followed. He felt the swaying motion and his knees began to shake. He looked down into the racing darkness below him, and could almost feel himself falling into it.

"I won't look down," he thought. Looking straight ahead, he walked on, gripping the shaky rail all the way.

The bridge shuddered as the wagon left it on the far side. One of the cows slipped with the change in the swinging of the bridge, and went to her knees. Hamlin cried out in fear, but in a moment the cow was up again.

When the last cow was off the bridge, and Doll and Queen were almost over to the other side of the river, Hamlin wiped his sleeve over his forehead. He was sweating, in spite of the cold, and so glad to be off that bridge that he could have run for joy, were it not for the slow-moving cows.

But he heard his father calling to him. "Hamlin!

Go back for Josh! I'll mind the cattle now."

The boy made himself turn around and walk back. The bridge was much steadier without the load on it, but that black serpent of a river still raced beneath it. He kept his eyes away from it until he reached the end of the bridge.

More of the ice had broken away at the edge. Would the bridge fall in before he could get back over it with Josh and the cutter?

He hurried to the cutter and took Josh's bridle rein.

"Come on, boy," he said.

Mrs. Garland flicked the whip over Josh's ears when the horse seemed unwilling to start. He gave in then, and followed Hamlin.

Step by step, they went nearer the bridge. Hamlin stepped onto the end boards, but Josh was not yet ready. He stopped. Hamlin tugged at the harness, anxious to get the cutter over before more chunks of ice broke away.

Suddenly, Hamlin's feet went out from under him. He reached for the handrail, but missed it and fell, face down. He heard his mother scream, and felt Josh's hoof touch his leg. The black serpent was

right before his eyes and he was grasping for the edge of the ice to keep from sliding into the blackness.

The bridge bounded up and down as Mr. Garland came running across it. He pulled Hamlin back and helped him to his feet. "Son, — son, are you all right?"

Later, Hamlin couldn't remember how he got across that bridge, but he remembered how his knees shook as he climbed the bank on the Minnesota side.

The rest of the trip that day was one icy hill after another, until they left the Mississippi Valley and came to the open flat stretches beyond. At night they stopped at an inn that stood near a mill dam in a little river. Hamlin was too tired to go to sleep quickly. He listened to the roar of the water over the dam until at last its song drowned out the remembrance of that black Mississippi water so near his face, and sleep came.

The next day, they headed southwest. It was farther and farther between patches of woods, with more and more of the open prairie. Just before dark, they reached another patch of woods.

"We're in Iowa now," Mr. Garland said. "Just after these woods, we'll see our new home."

It grew completely dark while they went through the woods. When they came out into the open again, Dick Garland pointed to a tiny spot of light about a quarter of a mile away.

"That's it!" he called back to his wife "We are almost there, Belle!"

On they went, slowly now, for the horses could hardly walk for tiredness. Hamlin tried hard to see what the house looked like, but it was just a dark shape against the snow. He could see that a beautiful big tree spread its arms over it, and that the light came from two, small square windows.

Dick Garland called out, "Halloo-oo, the house!"

A third shape of light appeared as the door opened. A man came out. "Is that thee, friend Richard?"

"Yes, Neighbor Barley!" Father called, and explained to Hamlin that Mr. Barley was a Quaker and spoke in the way that Quakers used in those days.

Hamlin was too sleepy to remember much about that evening. Mrs. Barley had good warm food for them all, and there was a bed somewhere for him and Frank. He slept through all the unloading of the sleigh the next morning, through the taking away of the Barleys' furniture and the good-bys.

When he awoke at last, he was covered with his own mother's quilts, in the bed in which he had slept all his life. The friendly old wooden clock was ticking away on the shelf, just as it always had in that other kitchen, and the big stove was back at its work of keeping the Garlands warm and cooking their food. Near it, his mother stood stirring up something that smelled of home.

"Flapjacks!" Hamlin said, and was out of bed.

A little later, he and Harriet and Frank went outdoors to explore the new world. The house was a log cabin, like those that Hamlin expected pioneers to live in.

"Oh, boy!" he said, and instantly short, stocky little Hamlin Garland, going on nine, became tall, slender Daniel Boone, scouting the frontier. Beyond the house, stretching for miles and miles, were white-blanketed fields, with here and there some dry stubble sticking up. Back of the house was the deep woods through which they had come the night before.

"Look, Harriet!" he called, pointing to the snowy yard. "Rabbit tracks! There must have been a rabbit ball here last night."

In a moment, the children were trying to follow in the rabbits' dance steps, laughing and happy again in this, their new home.

It was a magic world, the frontier where the woods left off and the prairies began.

Cabin at the Edge of the Woods

Each day the place seemed more wonderful to Hamlin, Harriet and little Frank. The log cabin was the heart of adventure. Hamlin, sleeping under the roof peak, didn't even mind when there was a little drift of snow beside his low bed in the morning. He hurried down to the warmth of the stove where Mother had a hot breakfast cooking. Soon he was outdoors getting water for the animals and breathing deeply of the nippy air.

When the morning work was done and breakfast eaten, he and Harriet always studied the tracks of the rabbits in the frozen dooryard, guessing how many had been there, how large they were, and trying to follow them to their daytime hideaways. The squirrels in the big oak tree that sheltered the cabin tried hard to chatter louder and faster than the children did.

"Here's a 'coon track!" Ham would call when they had checked on the rabbits, and he and Harriet would follow it as far as they could into the snowy aisles of the woods back of the house.

Once in a while they walked an hour through the woods to the village, or visited at the home of their neighbors, the Petersons, who had come to Iowa from Norway. Lars Peterson was twelve years old and seemed a very big boy to Hamlin. Whatever Lars wanted to do, Hamlin was willing to try.

"Let's teach these oxen to pull the sled and give us a ride," Lars said one day. The oxen were only a year old, and had never been taught to work. They kicked and bellowed, but after a while Lars got a yoke and harness onto them. After a few days, they even pulled a sled-load of firewood to the house. But one day they decided they were too young to work, and broke the yoke. The children were tired of working so hard for so little and turned to other things.

One day, Hamlin and Harriet heard a far-off sound that could mean only one thing.

"Spring is here!" cried Hamlin. "See the wild geese?"

In a great V, the birds winged their way from the south to the north. From then on, each day brought more signs of spring. When Hamlin went down to the little rock ledge north of the house to fill the water bucket from the spring that pushed out between the rock layers, he found it running faster each day and bubbling gaily into the brook that had been icebound all winter.

Spring brought wild flowers and fresh green grass to the prairie to the south and the west, but it also brought plowing time. With plowing time came trouble.

"I can't break this sod alone, Belle," Dick Garland said when he came in after a day in town. "I've found a couple of fellows who just got here from Norway. They can't speak English, but they can work. They'll be here in a day or two."

"Where will they sleep?" Belle Garland asked. "This tiny cabin is crowded with the five of us."

"They can bed down in the shed," Dick Garland said.

A few days later, the two big blond men arrived. The children watched them push and pull at the big breaking plow, sometimes riding on it to make it dig deeper into the heavy mat of grass roots. Doll and Queen pulled with all their might, but the roots were hard to loosen from the earth's grip.

Hamlin found it interesting to listen to the two men talk to each other, even though he could not understand a word.

"How do Doll and Queen know what they are saying?" he said to Harriet as they watched the horses swing right or left in answer to the shouts of the young men from Norway.

There were bushes and trees to be pulled from the new field that Mr. Garland was clearing, too, and here and there a large rock to be moved away.

"Some day," Dick Garland said, "I'll have a field where there is not a tree root to stop the plow nor a rock to nick it. I'll find a homestead out on the open plains, far from the woods."

The two helpers had not been there long when it was learned that the terrible sickness called small-pox had come with them. The girl who came each day to help Belle Garland around the house got it first. A day or two later, Dick Garland could not get up. Each day he grew worse.

Mrs. Garland was expecting a baby and it was a very bad time for her. One of the neighborhood women came in to help her. At night, Hamlin lay in his bed worrying about what he would do if his father died and he, Hamlin, became the man of the family when he was only nine years old. One night he had at last fallen into a deep sleep when he was awakened by his mother's crying out in pain. He heard Mrs. Briggs, the neighbor woman, moving about and speaking softly. A little while later, there was a new voice, and Harriet, Hamlin and Frank had a new sister.

In the morning, everyone was more cheerful.

"Your father is feeling much better," Mrs. Briggs told the children. "He'll soon be up and about, and so will your mother."

Somehow, the rest of them stayed well. The new baby was named Jessie, and she, too, did well. A day or two later, Dick Garland was outside, showing the hired men how he wanted the wheat seed planted.

"Now, Hamlin," he said when the seed had all been scattered, "it is your job to see that the birds don't eat our crop before it has even sprouted."

Great flocks of wild pigeons gathered as the men scattered the wheat seed. The birds swooped down to the ground, hungry for anything they could find in the spring months before nature had much for them to eat.

Mr. Garland took from its rack a double-barreled shotgun.

"You will soon learn how to use this, son, and you can't do any harm out there in the field," he said, handing the gun to Hamlin. "You're fast growing into a man. From now on, you must begin to do a man's work."

Hamlin was short for a nine year old, but he squared his shoulders as he took the gun. He marched off to the field with it, feeling like a soldier going to war. All day long he fought the battle of the pigeons, keeping the gun loaded and ready to bang out the moment the birds came back to the field. Young Frank followed after his big brother.

"Let me try it, Ham."

"No, Frank. Guns are for men. You are too small."

Frank settled down at Hamlin's heels until Hamlin's new standing as a man had to be exercised again.

"Get me something to eat, Frank. Bring a glass

of milk, too," he ordered. Frank obeyed. Soon he was back with cookies, warm from the oven, and a pitcher of milk.

"Here, Ham."

"Just a minute, Frank," Hamlin said in his new man's voice. He had just fired again. Carefully he loaded and capped the gun and laid it on the ground, pointing away from himself and Frank. "In a couple of years, I'll teach you how to use this gun," he said. A moment later his mouth was too full for him to say anything.

After a few days, there was not a pigeon to be seen. But by that time, the little striped-back gophers were trying to stuff their cheek-pockets with the wheat seed. Day after day, Hamlin marched around the field with his shotgun over his shoulder. He listened for the sharp little whistle that would tell him that a gopher was about to have a feast.

"Cute little things, aren't they?" Harriet said. "It is too bad Father wants them shot."

Hamlin softened a bit, for the gophers were fun to watch. But then he saw busy paws and teeth doing away with the grain that meant bread and butter to the Garland family, and his heart hardened.

"Bang!" rang out the shotgun, and its peppery load sent the gophers scurrying back to their holes.

When the seed had sprouted and grown an inch or two, Hamlin could go off guard duty. But there was news of something else to do.

"School's opening for the month of May!" came word from Lars Peterson.

Harriet, Hamlin and Frank took their tin dinner pails with them in the morning and walked westward over the prairie a mile to the little schoolhouse. There were children of all sizes and ages in the one room, from little fellows of five to one girl who was as old as the teacher. Many of the children were from families who spoke only Norwegian at home, and sometimes Lars or other Norwegian children who knew both languages had to help the teacher and pupils understand each other.

Mother and baby Jessie were home alone most of that month, for Dick Garland went looking for that homestead on the prairie, far from the woodlands, while the crops were growing. When he came home again, his gray eyes were bright with dreams.

"I found it," he said. "There is a place that we can have with a house on it, right next to a quarter section that has never been homesteaded."

The Garland children stared at each other.

"Must we move again?" Hamlin asked.

"Yes, son. Don't you remember that man from England who came by a month or two ago? He bought this house and land. Now we can move on to the best farming land in the country. You can see for miles and miles. Why, a man could plow all day without hitting a rock or a tree root. I've filed my claim on a quarter section."

During the War Between the States, President Lincoln had signed into law a plan by which settlers could have land almost free. All they had to do was to pay a few dollars for filing a claim and then build a home on the land and farm it. If they were still there in five years, the land was their own.

Mrs. Garland had been very quiet. Now she said, "When must we move, Richard?"

"As soon as the crops are in, Belle. I'll build you a fine new home, my dear. You will like it out there."

The summer went by in blackberry picking, exploring the woods and playing with the neighbor children. Hamlin had to help with some of the cutting of the grain and with threshing it, but there were many hours for him to enjoy himself. But at the end of August, moving day came again.

This time the wagon bed was on wheels instead of sleigh runners. But it was loaded as before, and again Dick Garland's voice, full of the drive and excitement of a true pioneer, called out "Forward march!"

It was much like the journey that had brought them to the cabin at the edge of the woods, except that the weather was warm and there were now four Garland children instead of three. Hamlin looked back at the log house sheltered by the big oak tree and wondered how any other place could ever be as wonderful. Then he turned his eyes to the west.

On and on they went. Each mile the houses were farther apart, and each mile had more land which had never been plowed. On the second day, the sun dropped below a line unbroken by a single rooftop. The wagon followed a narrow trail between two seas of wild oats and waving blue-joint grass. There was no sign of animal life except for a hawk soaring gracefully against the blue sky.

The horses' heads hung low, but still the pioneer

father kept them moving on to the west. Dick Garland seemed to grow taller and his shoulders straighter the farther west they went.

As darkness came, they reached a stream. Hamlin helped lead the horses and the cattle to drink. Then he lay down to rest in the buggy. The sound of the rippling water was a lullaby, and he did not even know that his father was harnessing the horses again. The next that he heard was his mother's voice saying, "Wake up, children! Here we are."

He opened his eyes to the blackness of night. In a moment he made out the dim shape of a house. It was to be the third home in Hamlin Garland's short life.

Plowboy of the Prairie

"I never thought you could see so far and see nothing," Hamlin said the next morning. He and Frank had climbed to the roof of the dreary little house that was their new home.

"There's something," Frank said, hopefully. "See — over there."

Hamlin looked off to the west where Frank pointed. There was the shape of a house, breaking the line where sky and earth met.

"We aren't the only people out here, but it sure seems like it," Hamlin said. Later he learned that the house he could see was the stone house of a family named Button.

Their own house looked sad in the morning light. The pine boards of its sides were so loose they rattled in the wind, and they had never been painted. There wasn't even a decent shelf on which to put the clock in the one room that would be kitchen, sitting room and bedroom. The picture of General

Grant seemed too fine for the cracked, poorly plastered walls.

Dick Garland didn't see how dreary the place was. "This is only a rented farm," he said. "We'll tighten up the house for the winter, but soon we'll move into a new house on our own homestead, as soon as we can get it built next summer."

His eyes turned away from the rented farm to the endless stretch of waving grass to the south, and they became bright with his plans. "Wonderful, wonderful earth, boys — without a tree root to stop a plow, and it will be ours."

The boys did not share his pleasure in the fact that there were no trees. They remembered the lovely oaks around the log cabin home, and the woods not far away where they had had so much fun. This place would have seemed much better to them if only a few of those trees stood near.

The boys sat on the roof trying to see to the edge of the prairie. "It just goes on and on," Frank said.

But Hamlin, looking far off to the southwest, had seen something he would never forget. He pulled at Frank's sleeve. "Look, Frank! Away off there —"

There was a little rise in the land, and suddenly

standing out against the sky had come a dark pony. Its white mane and tail flew out as it ran. After it came a great herd of wild horses, sweeping towards the boys and then swinging away again, their hoofs drumming out an untamed song of power and joy and freedom. This great unfenced world was theirs and no man had ever stopped them.

Frank and Hamlin sat on the roof, watching until the last flying tail had disappeared and the drumming of the hoofs was faint and far off. Then Hamlin could hear the pounding of his own heart, beating in a new excitement. This was the secret of the plains; this was what his father had felt as he turned his family away from the safety of the home in Wisconsin and led them farther and farther from the comforting shelter of the trees.

A few days later, Mr. Garland said, "Hamlin, I think you're big enough to handle Doll and Queen for the fall plowing. Neighbor Button and I are going to board up the house for your mother so that we can keep the wind out. We've got to have that field ready for spring planting. All that stubble has to be turned in to rot over the winter."

The people who had lived on this place before

had "broken" this land, cutting into the heavy sod and turning it well, but they had been gone from it a year and wild buckwheat had taken over the fields. The plowing would not be easy. Hamlin was ten years old and short for his age, but to have his father think him enough of a man to handle this job made him feel twice as tall as he was.

"Gee, Ham, can I help?" eight year old Frank asked.

Hamlin looked down at Frank from his new height. "This is man's work, Frank. You're much too small. But I'll let you bring me some water now and then."

The next morning, Hamlin threw the heavy harness over the big horses' backs. He could hardly reach the strap that stayed on top of Doll's back. But as he fastened the buckles, his touch was sure and his voice was the voice of a master.

"Back up there!" he shouted when at last the team was ready. The big animals did as he ordered and backed into place before the plow. Hamlin fastened the plow straps. Then he pulled his old straw hat a little more firmly onto his head, and wound the guide lines around his body and across his shoulders so that his hands would be free to hold the plow handles. With a loud "Giddap!" he set the horses moving forward into the field.

The iron plowpoint bit into the ground and the horses steadied themselves after the sudden backward pull. Hamlin felt tall and proud. It took a man to guide a plow and the fact that he could do it removed him forever from the small boy's world.

But the plow handles were placed for the grip of a man. They were even with Hamlin's shoulders instead of his hips, and he had to hold his arms high. The team had not pulled through more than twenty feet of the heavy earth, wet underneath from the rain that had fallen a few days ago, when the first ache began to come into the boy's shoulder muscles. Hamlin was finding that holding those plow handles steady was almost more than he could manage.

The row stretched ahead for a quarter of a mile. By the time the first turn was reached, Hamlin wished he could change places with Frank, who was trotting along behind him, stopping now and then to watch a nest of field mice, suddenly forced to give up their home, and scurrying for cover in the stubble.

At the turn, the plow pulled to its side. It was all Ham could do to pull down the handle. The ground was low there, too, and the wet soil balled up between the iron blade that cut into the earth and the curved plowshare that turned it over. He had to stop the team to clear the mud away so that the plow could bite in again.

By the time he had been up and down the field once, the September sun was growing hot. Hamlin pulled a bandanna from his hip pocket and wiped his face. He took off his hat for a moment and his hair was dark with wetness.

"Bring me a dipper of water, Frank," he ordered, and Frank scurried off to the well that was near the house. Harriet, in the yard to hang up baby clothes to dry, waved a greeting to the plowboy, and he felt less apart from his family.

The cool water tasted good. Hamlin gave Frank the empty dipper, wiped his mouth on his sleeve as he had seen the hired man do, and then took hold of the plow handles again. Blisters already had formed on his fingers and the inside of his thumbs.

This time Frank chose not to follow him. Hamlin guided the team so that the plow cut close alongside

the first row. It ran smoothly most of the time, with a satisfying ripping sound as it cut through the roots and turned up the rich, black earth. Hamlin saw what his father meant about this prairie soil. Plowing in Wisconsin had meant stopping often to clear rocks away or dig out old sprouting tree roots even after a field had been cleared. Hamlin didn't see a stone larger than a walnut in the whole quarter-mile row. There were no roots larger than those of the grasses and weeds to stop the plow.

Frank brought him cookies and milk about ten o'clock. One dragging hour later, Hamlin thought it must be noon. He did some arithmetic in his head and figured that he had followed the plow five miles so far. He whistled to make the time pass faster. He looked at the fluffy clouds, imagining them into sheep curling up for a rest or fat men lying on their backs with legs crossed. And still the noon dinner bell did not ring.

Hamlin began another round. He would try singing to pass the time and help him forget how hot it was and how his muscles ached.

"Cheer up, brother, as we go
O'er the mountains, westward ho — " he sang,

but his voice sounded small in the great outdoors of the prairie.

The song reminded him of the adventures neighbor Button liked to tell about going to California for gold, so Hamlin tried to imagine Doll and Queen were pulling his covered wagon. But that didn't work, for Doll and Queen suddenly stumbled and almost fell just as Hamlin had hitched the wagon for a day's adventure.

"Whoa!" he cried. Queen had caught her hoof in the harness as she tried to kick the flies off her underside, and Hamlin had to untangle the lines. The flies bothered him almost as much as they did the horses. Doll's tail switching into his face as he worked didn't help, either.

"Won't that dinner bell ever ring?" he said aloud after he had stopped five times in one row to straighten out the harness.

As if in answer came the "Ding, dong! Ding, dong!" of the bell that hung outside the door of the house. It was the sweetest music Hamlin had ever heard.

He unsnapped the harness from the plow and drove the team in for water and a rest. Then he went to the house and poured water into the basin on the bench beside the door. He swished cool water all over his head.

"That's better!" he said, and went inside to the dinner his mother had ready for him.

It was hard to go back to the plowing after the short noon rest. His muscles ached more than they had before he sat down to dinner. When he reached the field, he looked at the little strip of turned black earth that had looked so wide when he left it to go to dinner. He shook his head.

"Sure doesn't look like much! It will take me forever to plow this whole field," he said. Doll and Queen nodded their heads to shake off flies, but Hamlin was sure it was because they, too, were discouraged about the job. All three went to work.

The next day Hamlin could hardly raise his arms.

"Richard, do you really think he should plow again today?" Mrs. Garland asked. "Why not let him rest a day?"

"A soldier cannot rest until the battle is ended," Dick Garland said. Then his voice softened a bit. "It would be harder to go back to it tomorrow,

Belle. He will grow used to it that much sooner by working at it again today. He has to learn a man's work soon."

Mrs. Garland glanced at Hamlin. His short body and hair that would not stay combed scarcely went with her idea of a man, but she did not argue with her husband.

So Hamlin, his whole body one giant ache, went again to the field. That day, and the next, and the next and the next.

The second week was a little easier. The raw places on his hands had grown hard skin over them. His muscles were hardening, too. Day after day, the plowing went on. With the end of September, the heat and the flies were less of a bother. And one morning early in October, Hamlin awoke to the steady pattering of rain on the roof.

He hurried into his clothes and sloshed over the muddy path to the barn.

"I can't plow today, Father!" he cried.

Mr. Garland was milking Old Spot. "I can see that you feel very bad about it, too, son."

The two laughed together as Hamlin pulled up another milking stool and set to work.

After breakfast, he got a paper-covered book he had borrowed from Neighbor Button. The faithful family stove was hard at work in this house, too, although it seemed to be lifting its rounded skirts to get away from the rough floor. One of its claw-shaped feet had a flat stone under it to keep the stove from rocking. Hamlin crawled under it into his nesting-place as he had always done, and spent a wonderful day reading *The Female Spy*, an unlikely and bloody tale of adventure in the War Between the States.

Too soon the rainy spell was over and the ground dry enough for the plowing to go on. October passed. November brought cold raw winds, and Hamlin's hands grew so stiff with cold that he could hardly unbend them to let go of the plow handles. He tried to plow with one hand in his pocket to warm it, but that did not work for long. And still the field was not finished.

One day, the great V's of wild geese flew over his head, heading south. Flight after flight went by. The next day the wind was bitter cold.

"Near zero tonight," Mr. Garland said as he came in from the barn after supper. Hamlin hoped the ground would freeze too hard for him to finish that endless field. But two days later, it was warm again, and the frost oozed out, making the soil stick to his boots in heavy lumps.

The first snow, around November tenth, found him still plowing, with the big wet flakes clinging to his clothes.

"Now he will let me quit," Hamlin thought.

But the snow did not last. Two days later, Hamlin was in the field again. Then the thermometer began to drop once more. It went down to ten degrees and stayed below freezing for three days.

Each morning, Hamlin asked hopefully, "The plow can't cut into this frozen ground, can it, Father?"

"We'll see," said Mr. Garland. After breakfast, he went outside and tested the soil with his boot. "The frost is not too deep yet. You can cut under it all right," he said.

It was hard work getting the plow to bite into the frozen crust, and Hamlin hated each cold hour of the work. The chill in his body seemed never to leave, even at night.

On the third morning of the cold spell, as Hamlin finished his hotcakes he said, "Please, Father, may I leave that last strip until spring? I don't have to plow again today, do I?"

Mr. Garland put down his fork and looked sternly at the boy.

"If it is at all possible to plow, you must do it. As long as an unplowed strip remains, the battle is not won. Now get out there and fight like a good soldier."

Hamlin swallowed the lump in his throat. As he arose from the table, he saw Frank crawling into his "nest." Without a word, the "soldier" took his coat, mittens, cap and muffler from the peg by the door and put them on. A few minutes later, he was throwing the hated plow harness over the horses' backs.

Clouds of steam came from the horses' mouths and the boy's as the three went to the field. Hamlin's feet slipped on the frosted lumps of ground as he drove Doll and Queen to the edge of the unplowed strip.

When the plow was in place, Hamlin pushed and shoved to get the point to break into the frozen ground. It slipped, time and again.

"Anyone can see we can't plow today," Hamlin

muttered. "But we've got to prove it." He lowered his voice to an imitation of his father's. "Can't give up until the battle is won, Hamlin. Get out there and fight like a good soldier."

Tears came to his eyes as he pushed and shoved at the plow point. The horses backed and tugged. Then suddenly, the point broke into the ground. It turned the soil for a few feet and then stopped again. Hamlin gritted his teeth, backed the team, and dug in again.

No crows cawed from the fence posts and no hawks circled the sky. Even the little gophers were staying in their holes that day. Hamlin felt all alone, more alone than he had ever felt in his whole life. He struggled on.

The wind blew stronger from the northwest, and Hamlin pulled his muffler around his chin. Icy bits of sleet struck at his face, and he worked blindly. He slipped and fell once, but he got up again. On and on he went, trying to turn away from the cutting sleet, slipping, sliding. The icy sleet turned to white, and soon it was snowing hard, dry flakes carried on a wind that cut straight across the prairie.

Hamlin could hardly stand up against the blizzard, but the harness lines around his body helped keep him on his feet.

"Keep on with the battle, Hamlin," he said between his teeth.

Back at the house, Dick Garland was busy with his hammer and saw, building a cupboard for his wife. Frank and Harriet were playing checkers with buttons on the red-checked tablecloth. Mrs. Garland sat in the old rocker, feeding baby Jessie. It wasn't until she finished and rose to take the baby to her cradle that anyone looked out the window.

"Richard! It's a regular blizzard outside! Is Hamlin still out in that field?"

Mr. Garland put down his tools. "Oh, I don't think so, Belle. He must be in the barn, unharnessing Doll and Queen. He'll come in in a minute or so."

But a few minutes later, Hamlin had not come in.

"Richard, he's only a child. Go help him unhitch that team. He must be frozen," Mrs. Garland said.

A few minutes later, Mr. Garland looked into the barn. Only Old Josh was in the horses' stall. He turned, alarm on his face, and headed toward the field, facing into the blinding blizzard.

"Hamlin!" he called, but the wind shot the word back into his face. He could not see three feet ahead, and he walked on in blindness. Snow was beginning to fill in the hollows between the rough dirt ridges in the plowed field, and he stumbled many times as he made his way toward that last unplowed strip.

He almost fell over the plow before he saw it, tipped over, with the point jabbed into the earth. Part of one last narrow unplowed row was left of that great field. Doll and Queen were standing quietly, heads bowed against the blizzard. There at his feet was Hamlin, face down on the ground, but one hand still gripping the plow handle.

Fear struck Mr. Garland with a greater chill than the storm sent through him. Then he saw that the boy was trying to get up.

"Son, son — " Dick Garland knelt down to help Hamlin to his feet. He saw the blood oozing from a thin line on the boy's temple, and a bluish lump rising around it. It was plain to see that Hamlin had fallen against the plow handle as the plow tipped over.

"I tried, Father — I tried to finish it like a good

51

soldier," Hamlin said. His teeth chattered and he sobbed.

Mr. Garland saw how small the boy was. He unwound the harness and picked his son up and turned toward the house with the boy in his arms.

"I'll be back for you, Doll and Queen," he said.

He bent enough to touch his rough cheek against Hamlin's.

"Even the best of soldiers has to retreat now and then," he said.

The next morning, Hamlin had only one chore to do after breakfast. He went to the barn to clean and oil the plow and the harness that his father had brought in after he finished that last part of a row. It was almost fun to do that work, even though his head still throbbed from his bad bump.

At dinnertime, when he pulled his chair out from the table, Hamlin saw something on the chair seat. It was the worn leather case that held his father's treasured medal. He picked it up, opened it, and saw the bright ribbons and beautiful bronze disk. He looked up at his father.

Mr. Garland said, "For bravery above and beyond the call of duty, son. It's yours, Hamlin. You're a man now."

He pulled his shoulders straight and saluted. Hamlin did the same. Then father and son grinned at each other, man to man.

Journey to the General Store

The last of the fall work had been finished. Wintry winds whistled across the snow-covered prairie, and even the coyotes found home the best place to be.

The wind moaned around the corners of the little pine-board cabin where the Garlands lived, and rattled the loose wooden shingles on the roof. Cold gusts shredded the gray clouds of smoke sent upward by the hard-working stove. Dim light shone from the two windows, like watchful eyes on guard against the prairie night.

Inside, the Garland family, all but baby Jessie, were gathered around the table with its red and white checkered cloth and the kerosene lamp in the middle.

Mr. Garland cleared his throat and looked from Harriet to Hamlin to Frank, and then came to rest on his wife's face.

"Well, Belle," he said, and his tone brought even Hamlin's eyes to his face, torn from his reading for the tenth time of the lady spy who was about to be shot. "School opens next Monday. I suppose we'll have to take these young ones to town and fit 'em out."

To go to town was something special in itself. Hamlin had heard about the wonders of Osage, but he had never been there. And to go to get new boots and books for school! It was enough to keep a prairie boy awake half the night with excitement. The lady spy was forgotten.

Early in the morning, Hamlin helped feed the horses and cattle and milk the cows. Mrs. Garland had a good hot breakfast ready, but the children were much too excited to eat. Who could think of eating?

There was not enough snow that week for the sleigh runners to be used on the wagon, but the horses found it harder going than if there had been a good covering of snow. The dirt road had frozen and thawed and then frozen again into rock-like ridges. Harriet, Frank and Hamlin were glad to have the new spring seat in the back of the wagon to sit on instead of having to sit on the floor and take the rough jarring. They had a buffalo robe over their knees and tucked in under their feet and around the edges. Baby Jessie rode in front with Mr. and Mrs. Garland.

They rode into town in good frontier style, not minding that their carriage horses were really plow horses. Doll and Queen shied a bit when a young fellow in a light buggy whipped his high-stepping horse to a gallop and passed the Garland wagon with only inches between the carriages. Dick Garland quieted them in a moment and walked them to the hitching rail in front of the town's largest general store. He knotted the reins around the rail lightly and turned to help Jessie and Mrs. Garland from the wagon.

"Here we are, children. Help your sister down, Hamlin."

Hamlin almost fell out of the wagon himself, for he was trying to take in all the sights of Osage. His father had told him that about twelve hundred people lived here, and he could hardly imagine there being that many people in all the world. True, Osage was not quite so big as La Crosse, Wisconsin, but on moving day they had not had time to look around in that city or to get out of the sleigh and walk on the board sidewalks.

It was almost too much for Frank. He held onto his father's hand, too shy to answer the "Hello, young feller" of one of the men who sat smoking their pipes outside the store. Hamlin and Harriet, following after their parents, tried to act as if coming to town were an everyday thing for them.

They went inside the general store. The air that hit them as they stepped inside was warm and heavy. There was a big round heating stove glowing in the middle of the room, and more men were sitting around it. There were counters and shelves and tables loaded with more things than Hamlin had ever before seen. But it was the smell that struck him first — a delightful smell made up of many things. It was a mixture of new cloth, leather, tobacco, kerosene, gingersnaps, coffee and codfish.

"Oh, look, Ham!" cried Harriet. On a counter was a big glass jar of red and white-striped peppermint candy. Hamlin stumbled over a keg of nails as he turned to look, but hardly felt the bang on his shin for seeing the wonders of the great store. Mr. Garland was speaking to the man behind the counter on which the candy jar sat. The storekeeper wore a striped shirt without a collar or tie, but with a gold

collar button to hold the neckband closed. He had on suspenders to hold up his trousers, and a great black apron over the bulging front of him. His sleeves from the wrist to the elbow were covered with slip-on half-sleeves of the same black cloth.

"Five cents worth of peppermint, please," Mr. Garland said to this important person, and the children's eyes almost popped from their faces. They had never before had candy. Each had a bulge in his or her cheek like so many chipmunks carrying nuts the rest of the time they were in the store.

It didn't seem strange to the children to see shoes and boots next to a barrel of salted codfish. Another open barrel held soda crackers, each about three inches square and quite thick. Near them was a smaller barrel of gingersnaps, and Hamlin leaned over them, breathing deeply of the wonderful spicy smell. There were two big shiny black tin bins with gold designs painted on them, and TEA painted in gold on the hinged lids.

"The tea comes all the way across the Pacific Ocean," Dick Garland told his children, and Hamlin was lost for a few minutes as a sailor on the tossing deck of a schooner as it fought a storm at sea. But he came back from his dream in a hurry when he heard his father say, "Over here, Hamlin. You need a warm cap."

The storekeeper was holding a round brimless hat that looked like black fur but was really a kind of cloth called plush. For a moment, Hamlin thought the storekeeper was going to push him right down through the floor as he pushed the cap down onto Hamlin's head.

"That's too small. The boy has a large head," Mr. Garland said, and the storekeeper yanked the cap off, leaving Hamlin's hair standing in a wild bushiness. He screwed a slightly larger one onto the boy's head with a heavy hand.

"That'll do," said Mr. Garland. "Now try the smaller one on the other boy."

Buckskin mittens were next on the list. After that came the big moment when Mr. Garland walked up behind Hamlin as he was admiring the cavalry boots lined up on a shelf like so many soldiers waiting for inspection.

"What color tops do you want, Hamlin?" Mr. Garland asked. Hamlin knew exactly what he wanted.

"The ones with the red tops and the gold moon on them," he answered.

"If they have some to fit you, that is what you shall have," said his father. By "fit" he meant a size too large, as all the clothes were that were bought for children. By the time they really fit, they were almost worn out.

The storekeeper pulled down the pair of boots Hamlin wanted. They were beautiful! Frank chose boots with blue tops, trimmed with a golden flag. His had copper-capped toes, as all little boys' shoes did, so that they would not wear out so soon. Hamlin was filled with a secret joy to see that his feet had grown so much that year that his boots had to be chosen from the young men's rack. No more copper-toed boots for him! He did a man's work, and it was only fair that his feet had helped him into man's clothing.

He held his boots to his nose, breathing deeply of that wonderful oily leather smell. It was even better than leaning over the apple or gingersnap barrels. He hated to give up the boots to have them wrapped, but he knew better than to ask to wear them home from the store. No one ever wore new things that soon.

"Now for schoolbooks," Mr. Garland said. "Belle, you had better come over here and help choose the books the children need."

Mrs. Garland had been helping Harriet choose new shoes. They had also picked out a length of cloth for Harriet's new school dress.

"What will they need, Belle?" Mr. Garland asked. Belle Garland pulled an arithmetic book off the shelf.

"Every boy must learn his sums," she said, "and it won't hurt Harriet to study arithmetic, either. It is time they had one of these."

Next she took down a McGuffey's *New Fifth Reader*.

"Harriet is ready for this, too. She went through the fourth in her last term. Hamlin can use the old fourth."

Mr. Garland was leafing through a geography book. "Time they both learned something about the world. We'll take this, too."

In those days, especially in the frontier schools, children brought whatever books they could get. The teacher worked out a way to teach them from the books they had. Almost every school in the whole Middle West used McGuffey's readers, so the reading

63

classes were quite easy to handle. There were very few geography or arithmetic books to choose from, and almost always the children showed up with the books the teacher expected them to have.

Mr. Garland saw little Frank running his finger over the smooth, deep gray face of a slate. Its wooden frame had a bright red felt edging glued to it.

"Yes, Frank, you may have a slate on which to write your letters as you learn them," Mr. Garland said. "And Hamlin and Harriet may have new slates, too. A fresh new slate may help to keep your thinking clear as you do your sums on it."

The slates and the thin gray slate pencils were added to the bundle. Hamlin already had decided just where he would carve his name on the slate frame, and in what kind of letters he would do it.

As far as the children were concerned, the shopping ended there. Mr. and Mrs. Garland had a few more things to buy, but they were everyday things like salt and sewing thread and a couple of pounds of the square, hand-made nails people used in those days. While these things were being bought, Hamlin was busy reading all he could of a paper-covered book with a picture of Wild Bill Hickok on the cover.

All the way home, he sat with the package that held his new boots held tight in his arms. He could smell the lovely leather smell through the wrappings, and it awoke new dreams in his mind. He was riding to the west with Wild Bill. The golden moon on the red tops of the spurred boots he wore stood out against the sides of the great white horse he rode. His hair was no longer a wild mop on his head, but a beautiful shoulder length of flowing smoothness, like Wild Bill's. He fingered the buffalo robe on his lap and in a moment he and Wild Bill were closing in on a great herd of the shaggy beasts.

"Here we are, children," Dick Garland said. "Whoa, Doll. Whoa, Queen. Mind how you hold onto those bundles."

And there was the plain gray pine box that was home, instead of the adobe ranch house that he shared with Wild Bill on the trips they sometimes made in from the wilderness. The hoof beats were only those of Doll and Queen, anxious to get into the stable for some hay after their long trip to town and back. And the buffalo bellows were only Old Spot, Daisy and the others calling out that it was time for them to be milked.

Hamlin took the new boots into the house, un-wrapped them, admired their unscuffed newness and the beauty of the red tops, and took one long last sniff. The new dreams that had come with the boots would have to wait. He went out to help with the milking.

Pioneers Against the Prairie

School days did not last long for Hamlin. Three short months were all that a farm hand could be spared. In March, the new school boots were put away and Hamlin put on his heavy old farm boots.

"Back to your field, soldier," said Mr. Garland. "We have two farms to handle this spring. Besides farming this place, we've got to break sod on the homestead and build us a house. Your first job is to get that quarter section you plowed last fall ready for planting."

Hamlin sighed. Being a man wasn't much fun, and he envied Frank starting off to school each morning.

He began again the days of walking behind Doll and Queen. This time he was harrowing the ground, breaking the lumps left by the plow into fine dirt that seed would grow in.

"Well, here goes," he said to Doll and Queen as the three of them headed for the field the first morning. He expected it to be as it was in the fall, a long, hard dull job.

But it was different. He breathed deeply of the air.

"Springtime! Funny, but I never noticed that you could smell it coming," he said. "And do you hear that, Doll and Queen?"

Off in the wild grass at the edge of the field the prairie chickens were putting on their daily show.

"Boom-ah-boo-oom! Boom-ah-boo-oom!" Hamlin heard as he fastened the harness lines around his body. He stretched his neck to see the roosters doing their dance, and hurried Doll and Queen along the row to draw closer.

"You ought to come out with me some morning and see it," he told Frank that night. "Those crazy roosters thump and boom and strut around, putting on a show for the hens. They leap into the air, as if they were trying to fly but their wings won't work. Down they come and then they strut around like kings of the roost.

"And while they're strutting, that big orange balloon thing on their throats gets bigger and bigger. When it is about to burst, they jerk and leap and let out that great big boom that you can hear away up here in the house. You should have seen the fight that two of the roosters had this morning, Frank! Feathers flew like someone had popped open a pillow."

Frank was supposed to be studying, but he could not keep his mind on his schoolbooks. "Gee, Ham," he said, "do you think Father will let me stay home and do the harrowing? I'd like to see that show instead of going to school."

Hamlin looked very serious and shook his head. "Don't you do it, Frank. I'd a lot rather be in school any day than follow Doll and Queen around that field. You're lucky to be able to stay in school. I'd trade with you any day, prairie chickens and all. Besides, there's nothing going on at all in the afternoon."

All through April, Hamlin harrowed the field. He saw the wild geese fly back north, and the fresh green of springtime come to the prairie. Each day there was new growth to see, new wild flowers to bring home to his mother at noon, and new signs of the little animals of the field building nests for their new families. May came, and Hamlin finished the job.

He stood beside his father to show him the field ready for planting. There was something of that same glow in his eyes that lighted his father's eyes as he looked out over the open, endless plain.

"You did a good job, Hamlin," Mr. Garland said. "We'll plant it and then we'll break sod on the new land."

Uncle David, Mrs. Garland's big, cheerful brother, was opening a homestead not very far from the Garland place. He and Dick Garland were helping each other with the tough job of breaking the land that had never before been plowed.

The big "breaking plow" had a special cutting part on the front of it. There was a wooden platform there, for often the weight of a man was needed to keep the blade biting into the matted roots. Big, strong Uncle David handled the plow alone where the going was easiest, and he and Dick Garland worked it together when they hit a rough stretch. Most of the time, Hamlin's father worked ahead of the team, cutting brush and heavy weeds close to the ground with a great scythe. Hamlin had to rake the dry brush out of the way of the plow and burn it in a cleared place.

The first day that Hamlin was helping with the work, he was about twenty feet from his father when his father yelled, "Rattlesnakes, Hamlin! Look out!"

Hamlin saw his father striking at the ground with the scythe. He had come upon one of the many nests of snakes that lived in that grassy land that had never been disturbed. Again and again, Dick Garland lowered the scythe with a sure, fast blow. Back and forth he leaped, keeping a watchful eye for a snake that might be striking at him.

Hamlin saw a baby snake coming slithering toward him, and he chopped at it with his rake. He took a step backward, and stopped suddenly, for from behind him came a terrible sound. It was the warning rattle of a snake about to strike.

He wheeled. For an instant he stood frozen in fear. There, hissing angrily at him was a three-foot rattler. This one was no baby. Its fangs darted in and out.

"Get him, Hamlin! Hit him before he gets you!" cried Mr. Garland. He was running towards his son.

It happened all at once, then. Hamlin came to life and struck down with his rake. The rattler's head darted forward and the poison-carrying fangs shot out. At the same moment, Mr. Garland struck down at the snake just below the neck and pinned it

to the ground, cutting the creature in two.

Hamlin looked down. He felt a little sick.

"Did he get you?" Mr. Garland asked.

Hamlin swallowed hard. "Just my tough old boot."

After a while, Hamlin got used to fighting rattle-snakes and to watching for them. He and his father killed hundreds of them before they finished break-ing the sod in that quarter section.

"It will be finished today, won't it?" Hamlin asked one morning as he and his father went to the homestead land.

Dick Garland said, "Yes, we'll finish the break-ing today. But the battle isn't over yet, son. We must dig holes and set fence posts so that cattle can't get into our fields."

Hamlin sighed. It would be nice to be a boy again, instead of a man. August came and went in work, as usual. If there was nothing to do on the new land, there was a job waiting on the rented place, or on Uncle David's homestead. Mr. Garland was helping with the building of the new house, too.

In September, he said to Hamlin, "Time to begin to cross-cut the new field, son. Better start now before the fall rains begin."

After a few days, Hamlin began to wish the rains would begin. There had been almost no rain all through August and none so far in September. It seemed to Hamlin that the soil was blowing away on the ever-strong prairie winds as fast as he broke up the lumps left by the breaking plow. Fine bits of it blew into his hair and his eyes, and even between his teeth.

Hamlin noticed one afternoon that there was a smell of burned grass in the air, and it seemed to him that the air was not only dusty, but also smoky.

Back home, at supper, he asked about it.

"Yes, there are grass fires off on the unclaimed land to the west and the south," his father said. "The fall rains are so late in coming, and it has been such a dry summer, that miles and miles of prairie are burning."

As October began, the rosy glow stayed in the western sky after dark. Each day, the air was smokier than it had been the day before.

"The fires are coming closer every day," Mr. Garland said at supper. "I heard about a new house burning down on a homestead southwest of here.

The poor fellow that owned it couldn't get help in time to backfire around it. "

As Hamlin and his father drove Doll and Queen toward the homestead the next morning, they fought a strong wind all the way, and the skies were heavy with gray clouds.

Mr. Garland said, "That wind is bad today. It will sweep the fires right toward us, Hamlin. Unless, of course, those clouds open up at last and give us the good rains we need so badly."

Hamlin said, "What if it comes close to our new house, Father? What will we do?"

Mr. Garland looked as worried as the boy did. "We'll backfire, of course, the best we can. But these winds are bad. I hoped that tomorrow would be our moving day —"

It was just then that they saw a man on horseback coming along the road on the section line. He was waving his arms, and Mr. Garland knew that help was needed.

"Get on Queen, Hamlin, and I'll take Doll," he ordered.

As they passed the new house, they stopped just long enough to pick up two shovels. The rider was near enough then to call out, "Help needed at the McClintock place!"

"Your Uncle David's place!" Mr. Garland cried. "Hurry, Hamlin —" and he dug his heels into Doll's sides.

At last they rode into the bare new yard around Uncle David's house. As Hamlin jumped down from Queen's back, he almost fell, for the smoke choked him.

"Tie your bandanna around your face, son," Mr. Garland said.

Uncle David shouted, "We're backfiring, Dick!"

Fire will not cross a wide strip of land that has already been burned over. The trick in backfiring was to set fires that the men could control, and burn off the land before the wild fire reached it. Uncle David had tossed all the gunny sacks he owned into the watering tank near his new stable. Hamlin and his father joined the other two men who were turning up a line of dirt around the edge of the yard making a stopping line for the backfire that Uncle David was starting.

Hamlin's heart pounded as he dug, watching the

fire sweep through the grass toward him, first in little tongues, then in a sheet of flame.

"Dig around the barn!" the men yelled.

But the fire came too fast. The men beat at the ground with the wet gunny sacks, but the wall of flame closed in on the barn. Uncle David hurried into it to lead out his frightened horses. Hamlin helped pull out the new buggy and carry a few tools and buckets to a safe place. The men turned to keeping the tongues of flame away from the house.

When it was over, the men were hot, tired and blackened with soot. Quietly, they left to go to their own homes, thankful that the great wildfire had turned back on itself and there would be no more fires to fight that day.

The next day the rains began as the Garlands were moving into their new house. That night, in his bed in the upper room with the wood-shingled roof not two feet from his head, Hamlin listened to the roaring of the wind and the driving rat-atat-tat of the rain. It was like the music of a thousand little drums, beating out the good news that the dry spell and the fires were over.

There were other bad times in those pioneer

years on the plains. In summer, sometimes the grass-hoppers and the locusts came through by the thousands, the hot winds blew the good soil off the earth, and the thunderstorms came with a fury of wind and rain and lightning. In winter, blizzards did their best to bury each man-made thing in great drifts of snow, and the thermometer dropped too low to read.

Hamlin, standing beside his father when another battle against nature had been won, felt a glow of pride in the waving sea of grain he had helped make possible.

He remembered the day that he and Frank had watched the wild horses, and how the openness of these plains gave them a freedom and life unknown in the wooded lands.

He said, "The fight was worth it, wasn't it, Father?"

Dick Garland's eyes lighted up in the old way in his weather-worn face, and his hand went up in the soldier's salute. "Right you are, soldier," he said.

The frontier was tamed when Hamlin was at last man-sized. He became a teacher and a writer. Many of the stories and books he wrote were about his days of growing up and pioneering on the plains.

Howard Finds His Claim

While Hamlin Garland was growing up, there were people in every state east of the Mississippi River wondering if they should go west to homestead. Iowa land was nearly all taken. All that was left to be farmed lay between the Missouri River and the Rocky Mountains.

In those years of the 1870's, families gathered around their kitchen tables and, in the light of a kerosene lamp, studied the maps of Kansas, Nebraska and the Dakotas.

"The homestead land is going fast. If we are ever to get free land, we will have to go soon," they said. "Just think! The head of a family may have one-hundred-sixty acres, just for farming the land and living on it for five years. It is almost too good to be true."

Far away across the Atlantic Ocean, in many countries of Europe, people were saying the same thing in many different languages. And many of them packed their trunks, bought tickets on the ocean steamers and came to America.

Hundreds of Americans and Europeans made their way to the unclaimed land. Here is the story of one young American who went to Kansas in 1877 to homestead land for his family. His name was Howard Ruede, and we know his story because of the letters that he wrote to his family who waited back in Pennsylvania while he built a home for them.

With a creaking of wheels, a last snort and a tired hiss, the little locomotive with the big, funnel-shaped smokestack settled to a stop alongside the station at Kansas City, Missouri. A young man, in city clothes and carrying a suitcase made of carpet material, stood ready to get off the train. Two other young men, both a little older and huskier than he was, were close behind him.

"Kansas at last!" said the first young man, whose name was Howard Ruede.

The train conductor said, "Not yet, young feller. This here's Kansas City, Missouri. Kansas begins just west of the city, across the river."

"Well, let's get on the next train and get on to Kansas then," said Howard.

But it was six o'clock that evening, ten hours

later, before the three of them found seats in one of the crowded coaches taking homesteaders into the government lands. Then at last they heard the puffs and chugs that meant the train was starting, and felt the jerk of the car as it began to move.

"Hurray!" cried Howard and his two friends, Jim and Levin. Others in the car joined them. "On to Kansas!"

They were sure they would soon be flying across the Kansas prairie in the night. But at the state line, the train stopped. For an hour they waited there. Soon the air was stuffy and too hot, but there was no way to turn off the heat from the pot-bellied, coal stove that stood in place of one of the seats half-way down the car.

With much shouting and waving of lanterns, the train crew was adding freight cars to the train. The whole train shuddered with each bang that marked the addition of another car. The passengers, almost asleep, jumped, and then let their heads droop again. The dim light of the hanging kerosene lamps made crazy dancing shadows that slowly settled into stillness. Then another bang would come, the train-men would shout as they dropped the "pin" into place to lock the cars together, and the people and the shadows would come to life again.

Many of the cars that were added were empty cattle cars, being taken out to the places where the railroad met the cattle trails from Texas. At last they were all hooked on, and the journey began.

But the train could hardly be said to "fly" across the plains. At six in the morning, the tired, stiff people found they were only 118 miles from Kansas City, at Manhattan, Kansas. Some of the would-be homesteaders gave up there, got off and waited for a train back east.

On they went. The train stopped to pick up some passengers and Levin hurried to the car door.

"Where are you going, Levin?" Jim called after him.

Levin didn't answer, and his friends saw him running from the train as they looked out the window.

"Do you think he changed his mind about home-steading?" asked Howard. "The train is starting up again."

"Here he comes!" said Jim, who was looking out the window.

Levin came back into the car, panting and holding something in his hand.

"Look here, boys! I've brought you your first handful of Kansas soil," he said.

As Howard rubbed some between his fingers, his dream came alive again. It almost had been lost in this crowded car, with tired children whining, a sick baby screaming, and with cross, tired people complaining of how their muscles ached. He turned to look out the window, trying to imagine how his "claim" would look. Even through the dusty glass he could see the rolling land, dotted with a lonely house here and there. The grass grew thick, already beginning to show a little of the green of springtime. Here and there a row of bare-limbed trees showed where a river wound its way eastward toward the big Missouri.

"The land goes on forever," he said to his friends. Back in Pennsylvania, he had never felt the openness of the country, nor had he any idea how large the United States really was.

He turned back to the window. Now and then a frame house marked the heart of a farm, and once in a while there was a home built of stone. But mostly the houses were of a kind he had never seen before. "Soddies," they were called — houses built of blocks of matted grass roots and dirt.

"No soddy for me," Howard thought. "I'd like one of those stone houses on my homestead. That is what I shall build."

As the day went on, he saw another kind of house. It looked as if it had been built for midgets. It was a sod house that rose only two or three feet above the ground.

"That's a dugout," said Jim. "You dig a hole in the ground so that you don't have to make high walls. You cut some steps down into it, put in a door frame at the bottom of the steps, and you've got the easiest kind of house to build out here where wood is so scarce."

"Doesn't look like much of a house to me," said Howard. "I can't imagine asking Ma to come out here to live in a hole in the ground."

He went back to his dreams. He would build his fine house, plow some land and get in a crop, and then write home for Ma, Pa, Ruth, Syd and Bub to join him. Bub would grow up to be a real man out here in all this fresh air, not thin and pale like his older brothers were from their long hours of working at the printing office in Bethlehem. Ma could have a garden, and sit out in the shade in the afternoons. Shade? Well, he'd plant some trees right away, and soon there'd be shade for the stone house.

He reached into his pocket to make sure his purse was still there. It would be awful if he lost his money. All he had was what was left of his seventy-five dollars savings after he'd paid the cost of the trip. His ticket had been $23.05, and he'd had to buy some food. But fifty dollars should be enough to last until he could get work in a printing shop and earn more. Everyone said there was plenty of work in Kansas for a willing young man.

It was night again when the conductor called, "Russell! Russell!"

"Here we are, boys," said Jim, and led the way to the end of the car.

That night they slept well in a room at the Russell House. It felt good to stretch out and to have an end to the shaking of the railroad cars. They had been riding for three days and three nights without a chance to lie down. From Russell there was no railroad to the frontier town of Osborne, forty miles to the north. It was near Osborne that other people from Bethlehem had settled, and it was their letters that had sold Howard and his friends on the idea of going to Kansas to homestead.

In the morning they had to find a way to get to Osborne.

"I found a freighter who'll take us for one dollar each, and carry the trunks, too," Howard reported soon after breakfast.

Levin said, "That's for us. The best I could find was a teamster who would take us for $3.50 each and extra for our trunks. When do we start?"

"Right away," said Howard. "But the driver said we should buy some grub to take along."

Soon they were on the way. They rode until evening and stopped overnight at a log house, where Howard slept on the floor, rolled in a blanket, for the first time in his life. At noon the next day they reached Osborne.

It was just a little row of houses strung along one street. The prairie reached right up to the houses. The freight wagon pulled to a stop in front of a house marked CITY HOTEL.

Mr. Keever, the hotel keeper, came hurrying out

to make them welcome. He showed the three young men to a room, brought them towels and a pitcher of fresh water, and told them dinner would be ready in a few minutes.

"Journey's end," said Howard, "and I'm feeling better already. All we have to do now is find our claims and start building and plowing."

The next day, they went out to see some "claims" that were not far from Osborne, but those they saw had been partly homesteaded by other men. There would be a fifty dollar charge to get title to them.

"No use talking about it," Howard said. "I haven't got fifty dollars to my name."

They moved from the hotel out to the home of a man named Schweitzer where they could stay for less money. Howard was pleased to see that Schweitzer lived in a stone house, such as he hoped to begin building the next week.

"Is it hard to build a stone house, Mr. Schweitzer?" he asked.

Mr. Schweitzer shook his head. "Anyone who is willing to work can do it. There's a stone quarry not far from here, and when you break out the stone it cuts into blocks very easily. Hardens up after it's been out of the ground a few weeks. It lays up easily, too. Anyone who has a mind to can do it himself."

That night Howard wrote a letter home. He was in good spirits. "I guess by the next time you get a letter from me, I will be settled on my claim," he wrote.

During the next few days, Howard went into a dugout for the first time. He was surprised to see that, inside, plaster had been spread over the earth walls. It was whitewashed, and the room seemed quite pleasant.

"One thing about these dugouts," the owner said, "that prairie wind can't get into them."

"But isn't the dirt floor wet most of the time?"

"See for yourself. Dry as a bone."

Howard saw that it was dry, and swept smooth.

"I'd like a stone house, just the same," Howard said. "I think my mother would like it better."

"That would be nice," said the dugout owner. "But have you got a team to haul the rock to your claim?"

Howard hadn't thought of that. "No. How much does a team cost?"

"Good pair of oxen will cost you from eighty to one hundred dollars."

Howard fingered the purse with its little roll of money in it.

"I guess I could build a dugout first and then build the stone house for my family," he said.

By week's end, Howard had found his claim. Mr. Schweitzer, who was known for his kindness to newcomers, took the three young men to a place where there were three claims in a row, none of them taken as yet. Howard took the first quarter section, Levin the one west of it, and Jim the third one. There was not a single tree on any of them.

"See all that buffalo grass?" Mr. Schweitzer asked. The land stretched out, rough with the reddish brown, dry, tough grass left from the last season. It had never been plowed, and when Howard bent to pull some of the grass, it held on as if its roots went to the center of the earth.

"Buffalo grass means good soil," Schweitzer said.

Howard stood for a few minutes, picturing the stone house with its lovely trees around it, and the buffalo grass changed to fields of growing corn and wheat.

"When is it best to plant trees here, and where do you get them?" he asked.

Mr. Schweitzer shook his head. "Setting out trees is pretty hard. They dry out, unless you have a good wet summer. They often die in the hot winds, too. Now, I started my orchard from peach seeds we saved. That way, you have a better chance of getting the trees to grow."

Howard added a year or two to the time in which his mother could be sitting under the trees, but he would get them started soon. His dream took shape again, and that night, as he slept in Mr. Schweitzer's comfortable house, he saw his own claim as a lovely farm with a fine house sheltered by great trees. Ma would live out her days in happiness.

At Home in a Dugout

"We'll build your house first, Howard," Levin said. "All three of us can live there while we build the other two houses."

"I'd like to build it near the draw," Howard said.

Levin asked, "What do you mean — the *draw?*"

"Haven't you heard the folks out here use that word? That's what they call the little gullies where the water drains off the land after a rain on its way to the creek. There's a draw at the corner of my land. It runs on down to Kill Creek."

"Why do you want to build your house near it?" asked Jim.

"Because they say you can find water just a few feet down in a draw."

Jim nodded. "Hadn't thought about having to get water, but you sure can't do without it for long. We'll have to take some water with us in a jug each day."

Howard said, "That was one of the two things the pioneers back in Pennsylvania had that we don't have. There was always a spring or a good stream nearby. And they had trees."

The nearest farm to Howard's claim belonged to a man named Snyder. The three young men had moved out of Schweitzer's house and into Snyder's. Mr. Snyder's home was a sod house.

Howard studied the way it was built. The walls were made of slices of buffalo grass sod about two to three inches thick and eighteen inches long by twelve inches wide. He saw that the wall had a double row of "sods" at the bottom, making it about two feet thick where it had to hold the most weight.

"Do you think I could build a house like this to last until I could get a team to use in hauling stone for a stone house?" Howard asked Mr. Snyder.

Mr. Snyder shook his head. "Takes more work than you'd think to build a house like this. Cutting all that sod takes a long time and a good sod-busting plow. Have you got one?"

"No, but maybe I could rent one for a while."

"Got a team?"

"No, — "

Snyder shook his head. "You've not got enough

money to pay the cost of a man and team to cut all that sod, either, I suppose?"

Howard groaned. The problems were greater than he had thought. His seventy-five dollars had seemed a fortune back in Bethlehem. Now with almost half of it gone, he saw that he would need much more. He already had gone in to talk to the man who printed the newspaper in Osborne.

"A day or two now and then is all the work I can promise you," Mr. Barnhart, the printer, had told him. "But I am glad to know that there is a man nearby who knows the trade. I'll send word to you when I can use you, Howard. Good luck on your homesteading."

Howard had hoped he could work in the print-shop at least half the time, and use the other half on his farm. Levin and Jim had found a few days' work at a sawmill. They were both much stronger than Howard. Work he could do was hard to find.

Mr. Snyder saw how unhappy Howard looked.

"Tell you what, Howard," he said. "I'll bring my breaking plow over long enough to cut you enough sod for a dugout, and you can do some farm-work for me in trade. Is that a deal?"

Howard's face brightened. "It sure is, Mr. Snyder. I'll build a better house for my family when I have a team. A dugout will do for the three of us for a while, anyway."

Mr. Snyder said, "Take some advice from a man who's been here awhile. Don't buy a team until you have water. Hauling water for a team will break your back. They drink by the bucketful, you know, not by the cupful."

Howard said, "I've got a spot picked out for my well. You said you got water just six feet down in that little draw out there. I don't know why I can't do the same."

Mr. Snyder didn't look quite so sure. "Maybe, maybe," he said. "You never can be sure just where you'll find water."

Levin still had work at the sawmill when the last week in March began. Jim and Howard were ready to start the dugout on Wednesday. They went to Howard's claim, taking a borrowed shovel and a pick without a handle that Howard had bought. They had made a handle for it from a piece of wood Mr. Snyder gave them. Howard showed Jim the spot he had chosen near the draw, and they tried to dig into the earth there. They could not get through the buffalo grass roots.

"Over there, Howie," Jim said. "There's a patch of wild sunflower instead of buffalo grass. Let's see if we can dig there."

"I'll have to carry water farther, but this isn't the house I will bring Ma to, anyway," Howard said. So they marked off an oblong for the house in the sunflower patch.

Howard had thought he'd like a room about twenty feet long, until he tested the Kansas soil for digging. After he and Jim had loosened the first shovelfuls of dirt, he settled for a space ten by fourteen feet.

"We should dig it about six feet deep, Jim," he said. "Then if we build up about two feet of sod, it will make a room big enough for a man to be in without feeling so much like a mole in the ground."

They worked for a while, Jim breaking the ground with the pick and Howard shoveling away the loose dirt. Even though it was not yet April, the sun felt hot. By the time they had been digging two hours, so much sweat had run into Howard's eyes that he could hardly see. His hands were blistered.

His back and shoulders ached.

It was about eleven thirty when he stopped work and leaned on the shovel handle. "Jim," he said, "let's face it. This hole will take forever to dig. And when it is dug, what have we got?

"Look around you, Jim. Not much like Pennsylvania, is it? Almost flat — and not a tree in sight. Kansas is not what I thought it would be. I'm for going back to Osborne this afternoon and going home while I've still got the money to buy a railroad ticket."

Jim said nothing. He tried for the twentieth time to tighten the handle on the pick. When it was as tight as he could get it, he tossed it to one side.

"Look, Howard," he said then, "you're tired right now. This looks like an endless job. But think about Schweitzer's place, with its stone house and the orchard. He hasn't been here very many years, and when he started out his claim must have looked about like this one.

"Now, we'll go over to Snyder's, get some dinner and rest a bit. We'll fix this gol-darned handle so that it stays put, and then we'll come back and look at this hole again. And I miss my bet if it doesn't look to you as if we got a good deal done this morning!"

They walked the three-fourths of a mile back to the Snyder house. On the way, Howard stopped a moment, took off his left shoe and pulled off his sock. There was a big blister on his heel, and the holey sock made it worse. He walked on with one foot bare.

"That's better," he said. "Now I can face life in Kansas."

After dinner, Mr. Snyder fixed the pick handle for them. And Jim was right. The hole did look bigger when he and Howard went back to it.

"Snyder says to dig it a little deeper at one end than the other," Jim said. "That's so that the whole floor won't stay wet if a bad spell of rain comes and the roof leaks."

"Five feet deep at one end and five and a half at the other should be deep enough," Howard said.

Two days later he decided that five feet at one end and four and a half at the other would be deep enough. The digging was still very hard work for Howard, but he was getting used to it. Just the same, he was glad to take a day off when it rained.

"What happens in a bad rainy spell in a sod house like this?" Howard asked Mr. Snyder that day.

"We've got a good roof," Mr. Snyder said. "Same as you'll need for your dugout. You put a ridgepole from end to end, with the sods laid up to make the roof slope a little both ways from the middle. You lay plenty of poles from the ridge pole to the sod walls. Then you put cornstalks, sorghum stalks, grass — all the long dry stuff you can find over the poles. Next you lay a good tight layer of sod on top.

It takes a long, hard rain for a drop to come through on us."

Mrs. Snyder was frying potatoes for the men's supper at the big iron stove. At her husband's last words she gave him a look that spoke plenty, but all she said was one loud "Hum-m-ph!"

"Now, Ma," said Snyder, "you know this is a right good soddy."

Ma Snyder pushed the potato slices around in the big black frying pan. "Seems to me," she said, "that I remember having to hold an umbrella over this stove for about a week each spring while I cook your meals for you."

Snyder said, "I'll put another layer of sod on this spring, Ma. Someday we'll get us enough yards of muslin to make a ceiling over the room. Then you'll have the fanciest soddy in Kansas."

"If the walls don't fall in first," said Ma. "You need to put another brace on the south wall, Pa."

As was the case with most sod buildings, a lean had come into the walls of the Snyder house as the dirt in the sod "bricks" packed unevenly. It had pole braces set against the wall here and there to keep it from leaning more.

By Saturday, Howard decided that the hole was deep enough. It was four and a half feet deep at the deepest end and four feet at the other.

"Anybody that's real tall will have to stand in the middle of the room," he said. "That's enough digging."

Monday morning Howard set off to a farm he had heard about where there was wood for sale. It was on bottom land and had a creek running through it. About the only place that trees grew in that part of the country was on the bottom land along the streams. Mr. Smith had so much wood that he had a log house. He sold all the driftwood that came down the stream for firewood, and whole trees when people wanted them.

"What will Kansas people do for fuel when the wood is gone?" Howard asked Mr. Smith.

"They'll be shipping in coal soon, Howard. Someday there'll be a branch of the railroad right up to Osborne, and coal will come in by the car-load. Some comes in by wagon from Russell now. Won't need to worry this winter, though. I've got lots of driftwood piled up that came down in last spring's flood."

"I came to see if you had a ridgepole for my dugout," Howard said.

Mr. Smith walked over to a straight, tall burr oak tree, healthy and still growing.

"Here's one with a good straight trunk. You can cut a fine ridgepole from it. I'll sell you the whole tree for one dollar. You can get plenty of firewood out of it, a ridgepole, and poles for your rafters, too. Help yourself to the ax and cut it down."

Howard thought of how he would like to have that tree growing on his claim, if only there were a way to move it. It was too bad to cut it down when there were so few trees, but that seemed to be the only way to get the pole he needed. He picked up the ax, but was not sure how to go about cutting down the tree. He took one swing at it.

Mr. Smith said, "Haven't cut down many trees, have you, lad?"

"No, sir," said Howard. "In fact, I've never cut one down."

Mr. Smith reached for the ax. "Tell you what, Howard, I'll cut the tree down and haul the trunk to your place for an extra fifty cents."

Howard grinned. "It's a deal, sir." It was only

then that he realized he hadn't planned how he would get the tree trunk moved to his claim. Mr. Smith had a team of oxen and a wagon. Later in the day, they chained the log to the back of the wagon and the oxen pulled it to Howard's claim, dragging it along the ground.

"I should buy a team of oxen instead of horses, Mr. Smith," Howard said. "They don't go very fast, but they sure can pull."

Smith said, "That's not the only reason for having oxen. They can live on the buffalo grass you have on your land. You won't have to buy feed for them as you would for horses."

Howard's mind was made up. He would buy an ox team as soon as he could earn the money.

The next day Mr. Snyder came over with the breaking plow and his team. With Jim's help, he soon had a neat length of matted root turned up. With a spade, Howard began cutting the slice into lengths from eighteen to twenty inches long.

The boys had most of the things they needed to finish the dugout now, and soon they had a doorframe up at the foot of the steps Howard had cut into the ground and a frame set up for a small window. They laid up the "bricks" and filled the cracks with dirt from the pile left from the digging. Jim trimmed up a ridgepole from the tree trunk. It was soon in place with the rafters and cross poles tied onto it.

. The house was almost finished the night that Howard got a letter from home.

"Levin, listen to this," he said. He and Levin were sitting at the Snyder's round kitchen table, sharing the light of the one lamp in the room. "Pa thinks he should come out here and homestead, too. Pa can't do that! He's no farmer. What could he do out here? He's been out of work a long time, and he hasn't any money saved up. He just can't come here yet."

Levin said, "Tell him so, Howie. Tell him to stay where he has a roof over his head. Your brother Syd is making enough money to keep him going. It's a sure thing that if young fellows like us have trouble getting work, an older man would have a harder time. We both know now that it will be two years before our homesteads will give us a living."

Howard took out paper and pen and ink right away. "Tell Pa not to come unless he has enough

money to live on for six months," he wrote to his brother Syd. "Work is very scarce."

While Howard worked on finishing the house, Levin and Jim dug a hole in the draw, expecting to find water a few feet down. When they had a ten-foot hole, and still there was no water, they decided to try another place farther down the draw. Again, they found no water.

"We hit that layer of thin sheets of rock that break up easily — that stuff they call shale, Howie. All the farmers here say that if you hit shale it's no use going any deeper. You won't find water there."

Howard was worried. "A man can't get along without water on his place. What will I do, Levin?"

Levin said, "We won't give up yet, Howie. You just can't tell. I was talking to a fellow last week who said he dug through shale and went down about forty-two feet. Didn't find a drop of water. He tried again about fifteen feet from that hole, went down twenty feet, and there was plenty of water. Maybe we'll be lucky, too."

Howard moved into the dugout alone on Monday, April 16, 1877. Levin and Jim had work at a farm, and part of their pay was their "keep."

"Looks more like a hole than a home," Howard thought as he dragged his trunk down the dirt steps and into the dugout. It was all he had. There was no bed to sleep on, no stove, no table — not even a chair.

He sat down on the trunk and pulled his purse from his pocket. It didn't take him long to count his money, for most of it had been used to pay for his room and board. He had spent ten dollars on things needed to build the dugout.

"Two dollars and twenty cents!" he said aloud. It was all he had to his name. There was no chance to buy a cooking stove with that little bit of cash.

He went outside and picked up the unused sod bricks that were lying there. He took them into the house and made two stacks of them at the end of the room opposite the door. He had some sticks of green wood left from his oak tree, and with these he made a cooking top and braced a stack of cut sods to form a chimney. He was hungry when he finished.

He put dry wood into the space between his sod stacks and soon had a fire going. He put water, brought from the Snyders' well, into his one cooking pan and waited for it to boil so that he could make some cornmeal mush. Cornmeal was the only food he had.

More smoke came into the room than went into the sod chimney and out through the hole he had made for it in the roof. Smoke oozed out between the sods, and the air became blue with it.

The bluer the air became, the bluer Howard was. He wished he had gone back home while he still had the money to buy a ticket. No water, little food, almost no money, and worst of all, no work at which he could earn some money. What was he doing here in this hole in the ground? Was this the fine, brave new world of the homesteader?

He opened the door to let out the smoke and almost ran away from the place. Just then he heard the water boiling, and he turned back to make his cornmeal mush.

Later, with his stomach full, he made himself plan what he would do. His two dollars and twenty cents would have to be used for food. Maybe Mr. Barnhart would have work for him if he went into town and asked. In the meantime, there was more work to be done here. He didn't want to sleep on the dirt floor, so he made himself a bed of poles, overlaid with sorghum stalks left from the roof of the dugout and a quilt his mother had given him.

"Not much of a bed, but it will have to do," he muttered. He decided to test it, and fell asleep. He didn't wake up until he heard the roll of thunder about four o'clock in the afternoon. The wind brought a rush of rain. Howard sat on his trunk and watched the water darken the sods. It was a gloomy day, all around. And he thought he'd be so happy to move into his own house!

The next day he bargained for a ham, and a few pounds of dried beans. With the hundred-pound sack of cornmeal with only a little of it used, he could eat for a long time to come. Back home, he made a meal of ham and corncakes, well flavored with smoke.

After dinner he counted up his belongings and listed them in a letter to his family. He had one twenty pound ham, already with "meat flies" on it after only one meal cut from it. Besides the beans and cornmeal he had a tin cup, the two pails in which he carried water three quarters of a mile from Snyder's, one pottery bowl, one saucepan and one frying pan, a pie tin, a cracked cup to hold salt, and three each of plates, cups, saucers, knives, forks and spoons. For farming tools, he had a pick and a shovel and a length of rope.

He put down his pen after writing out this list and sat down on the lumpy bed. His heart sank. How was a man to plant corn without a plow to break the sod? How was he to plow without a team? How could he have a team without water? How could he do anything without money?

Big as he was, Howard was ready to cry. Instead, he coughed on a big whiff of smoke. He sat down on the bed again and his face twisted into a dry kind of smile. He spoke aloud.

"Oh, well — there's one good thing. The smoke helps kill the meat flies!"

All's Well That Ends Well

Howard remembered that day as the blackest of his life as a Kansas homesteader. His troubles weren't over, but never again did life seem so black. The next morning the sun shone. Howard set off for Osborne to see Mr. Barnhart about work.

"Yes, Howard, I can use you now, even if only for one or two days a week. Glad you came in," Mr. Barnhart said.

That was the beginning of better things. While he was in town Howard heard of a farmer who needed help now that the crops were coming up. He went to see him, and soon was out in the fields pulling sunflower sprouts out of the field of winter wheat. His pale city skin burned red and then turned brown. He let his whiskers grow, for without water it was hard to shave.

"You wouldn't know me if you saw me," he wrote home to his family. He wrote, too, that while things were better, he was not yet ready for Pa to come west. Pa had not given up the idea.

Even the problem of the meat flies on the ham was taken care of. His good friend, kind Mr. Schweitzer, traded him fresh meat for the ham, pound for pound, and told Howard he could take the fresh meat as he was ready for it.

Levin and Jim came to keep him company in the dugout between jobs. They used their time to try to find a place for a well. They borrowed a set of poles, one of which had a drill point on one end. This was turned and twisted down into the earth. The other poles were attached to its upper end as the hole was drilled deeper and deeper.

"With this water auger, we should be able to find a place for a well in a hurry," Levin said.

Howard hoped they'd be lucky on the first try. "I'm saving money for an ox team, and I'll be able to buy it soon if we can get water. My brother Syd is saving money for the team, too, so it won't take long."

He was anxious to get the team so that he could turn back a few rows of sod and begin to use his land a little. The sod had to rot through a season before it could be worked into the soil for wheat planting, but usually a settler raised "sod corn" the first year. He would go down a row of turned back sod, cut into it with an ax, and tuck seed corn into each cut. It didn't always do well, but there was usually enough of a crop to make it worth the work.

It rained while he was in town working for Barnhart at the end of April. He went from there out to a farm where he and Jim were to chop firewood for a day or two.

"Did you find water with the auger, Jim?" he asked.

"No," said Jim. "We kept hitting shale. Then we had to return the auger. Howie, I know you think it's silly, but why don't we try water-witching?"

"Seems like a waste of time to me. I don't believe that it could show us where water is," Howard said. But after they had borrowed the auger again and still had no luck, he was ready to try anything.

Old Jakey Gsell came over one day, bringing with him a forked branch of a peach tree. He held the branch out in front of him, a fork in each hand, and walked about on Howard's claim. Howard, Jim and Levin watched. Jakey walked back and forth for about fifteen minutes. Then the boys saw the

straight end of the branch drop downward, pointing to the ground.

"Here's the place, boys. Dig your well right here," Jakey said.

Howard dug at the spot where Jakey's stick had pointed. He worked four days, shoveling until he couldn't toss the dirt out any more because he was too far down into the ground. Then he had Levin lower the buckets on a rope. Howard filled them as Levin hauled them up.

On the fourth day he hit shale. "No use digging here any more, Levin," he said. "I didn't really think that peach stick could show us where water was, anyway."

The rains came again. "Funny," said Howard, "how we are getting too much water from above, and how I can't get any from below. If only we could get a good well — "

It rained as April ended and May began. By the middle of May, the farmers were beginning to worry about the soil being too wet for their crops. The rivers and creeks were beginning to flood. Howard went to town to work, and could not get back to his claim. He went out to Schweitzer's place when Mr.

Barnhart did not need him. All through May, the rain kept returning.

June began with a bright day. The rain seemed to be over at last. Howard was anxious to get out to his claim, but he could not yet get across the river. And then, the next evening, he got a piece of bad news. His dugout had fallen in. There had been too much rain for the sod bricks to hold.

" 'Tain't nothin' but a mudhole with a ridgepole and a few sticks of lumber in it, Howard," he was told. "You fellers must have let those walls slant inwards a little. That'll let them sink down until they can't hold up the rafters no more. Too bad, too bad — " and the friend went away, leaving gloom behind him as thick as the mud in the dugout.

That was Saturday night. Monday was the day the mail came, and Levin brought in a letter from home for Howard.

Howard read it quickly. Suddenly his mouth dropped open. "Levin, what date is today?"

"June 4. Why?"

"Oh, no! It can't be! Pa is taking the train west *tonight!* Now, when I haven't even got a house to take him to!"

He and Levin sat and stared at each other. At last, Levin said, "We can build another dugout, Howie. We know more about it now."

Howard slept little that night. The next day he went out to see a farmer who wanted a man to stay on his place as a full-time farm hand. Howard's muscles had toughened up enough now for him to be able to do the work. He got the job. But as soon as he had agreed to it, he began to worry about his father's coming and how he was going to get his own homestead going when he was not free to spend his time there.

Mr. Landes, the farmer, agreed to give part of Howard's pay in breaking the sod in one of Howard's fields, as soon as they had time and the ground was right. That made Howard feel a little better.

The first job they did at the Landes place was to move a frame house he had bought from a place a mile away. They took two wagons, with the wagon box sides taken off, out to the place where the house stood. Two other farmers had come to help with the work, bringing teams with them.

With much prodding with long poles and a great deal of yelling orders to each other, the men got the first side of the house onto the wagon beds. But there were sounds of nails pulling out and wood cracking.

"Hold it, boys!" yelled Mr. Landes. "We'll have to tighten her up in the joints or she'll fall apart."

They were all busily working when one of the men chanced to look off to the southwest.

"Look!" he yelled. "Run for cover!"

Sweeping across the rolling plain, rushing toward the men, were the blackest clouds Howard had ever seen. Far off, he saw a funnel-shaped cloud that dipped from the sky, reaching right down to the earth.

There was no time to waste. The men who owned the teams unhitched them and started them towards Landes' stable. Howard ran. He reached the stable just as the clouds opened. The rain turned to hail, and the wind had a wintry feel. The hailstones pounded on the straw and sod that roofed the stable and the building shook. Thunder, lightning and wind seemed to be battling each other to rule the earth.

It was all over in fifteen minutes. But there was no longer any need to work to move the house. The pieces that were left could be loaded onto the wagon beds if the men had the patience to hunt for the lumber after they turned the wagons right side up. Later they learned that in the path of the cyclone, heavy sod roofs had been lifted and people in dug-outs left with the rain pouring in from all sides.

A few days later, Howard was sent out to hoe the corn which was just sprouting. A man came walking across the field. Howard glanced at him, went back to his work, and then dropped the hoe.

"Pa!" he shouted.

The older man stared at Howard.

"Son! Is that you behind all those whiskers! I do believe you are twice the size you were when you left home, and you are burned like an Indian."

A few minutes later, when Howard had picked up the hoe and was again at work, they talked about how things were back home.

"Sure would like to see Ma," Howard said. "But we've got a long way to go before she can come. I'll not have her living in a dugout. She's got to have a good house if she is to put up with the weather here." He told Pa about the storm they had just had, and how the wind blew all the time.

Then he asked the question which had been in his mind all the time. "How much money have you got, Pa? We'll have to find a place for you to board."

Pa coughed. He cleared his throat.

Howard stopped working and leaned on the hoe, knowing somehow that what Pa had to say wouldn't be good news.

Mr. Ruede cleared his throat again. "Well, son, I had more than fifty-five dollars when I bought my railroad ticket. Of course you know that took almost twenty-five dollars."

"Yes, Pa. You should have thirty or thirty-five left. That will last a long time, if you're careful, and maybe you can get some light work to help out. Just how much do you have left?"

"Well, son, I had a bit of bad luck. When the train was stopped at Toledo, a man came up to me and started talking. He was very pleasant — nice fellow, he seemed. He asked me if I would mind giving him change for a bill he had. He said he needed it to pay back someone he had borrowed a dollar from. That was just as the conductor had called out 'All aboard!' and we were going back to our seats.

"Well, sir, I took out my money, pulled out the five dollar bills he wanted for change, and he snatched my purse instead of the change. He took thirty dollars! He jumped off that train just as it started rolling. Believe me, son, I tried to stop him. I yelled, 'Stop that man! Stop, thief!' But it did no good."

Howard sighed. Thirty dollars!

In a small voice, Mr. Ruede said, "I have just fifty cents left, son. But I am willing to work to help out."

Howard said no more. He stabbed at the weeds with the hoe. There was just one thing to be thankful for. His brother, Syd, had thought of sending the fifty dollars he'd saved for the team with Pa, but had changed his mind.

It surprised Howard to see how well Pa got along without money. People liked him and invited him to their homes for dinner. They loved to hear him talk, and one man offered him the job of teacher — when they got around to building a school. Pa and Jakey Gsell became close friends, and Jakey invited him to live with him, just for company.

Howard quit his job on the first of August, knowing he must get a house built soon. Barnhart wanted him to take care of the printshop for a couple of weeks while he went back to see his family in Iowa.

"Let's get that house started before I go to work, Pa," Howard said. "When it is finished, we'll write for Bub to come. He's big enough to do the work here at home while I work out and earn money for us all." Secretly, he was worried about leaving Pa alone in the wintertime. Bub wanted to come, and he would be both good company and a real help. Levin and Jim had broken up the partnership with Howard and gone their own ways.

They looked at the old dugout. "It will be more work to fix up than to build a new one, Pa," Howard said. He pulled the ridgepole, the lumber, and all his belongings from the mud. "We can use these again. You clean them up while I dig, Pa."

The new, stronger Howard found the work not nearly so hard as it had been in March. And because of all the rain, there was some water in the well in the draw that Levin had dug the first weeks they were in Kansas.

Whenever no one else was using it, Howard borrowed the water auger and took time out from house-building to try for water. Again and again he struck shale. He must have a well. Then he would be able to see his way clear to getting his homestead started. Mr. Landes was breaking three acres of sod for him, and he was putting seed potatoes into the land to help feed his little family that winter. He would be able to buy a stove for the new dugout with his earnings, as well as the other things they needed most, and have money left to put with Syd's money to pay for the team.

They had not found water when they moved into the new dugout on August 28. This one was much better than the first one, and Howard found a good stove for it.

Bub came when Howard sent for him. He was there soon after the dugout was ready. His young voice brought cheer into the dark room, and he seemed to think it was fun to kill the beetles and bugs that crawled out of the sod bricks.

"Sure good to have you here, Bub," Howard said. "Now if we could only get our well, we'd get that team, and begin the stone house so Ma, Ruthie and Syd could come."

But no matter where he dug, he could not get water. He and Bub worked together in hole after hole, hauling up buckets and buckets full of dirt. But no water could they find, even when they went down twenty-five feet.

Winter came. Howard worked in town much of the time, earning all he could. Syd sent the money for the team, and one day Mr. Schweitzer told Howard about a team of young oxen that was for sale at what he thought was a good price.

"Sam and Billy aren't very big, but they're strong and healthy, Howard. They'll make you a good team," he said.

Howard went out to see Sam and Billy. Even though he would have to haul water for them, he bought them, and a wagon, too.

"Makes me feel as if I'm getting somewhere to own a team and a wagon," he said. "We can't haul stone for a house without them. And I want to start that stone house for Ma soon."

He drove the outfit home, and he and Bub built a stable of poles and straw.

"Now we'll try again for water," Howard said. "I feel lucky."

He felt so lucky that he went to the quarry, cut stone to line a well, and hauled it home on his new wagon. Then he began to dig. He hit shale as before, but something told him to keep on digging.

He dug three feet more, chopping at the shale with his pick while Bub emptied the bucketloads of it. And suddenly there it was — a little pool of water.

"Hurray!" he yelled, as the pool grew larger and spread to fill the bottom of the hole. "Pa! Bub! We've got us a well!"

Pa grinned. "All's well that ends well, Howard," he said.

Howard didn't mind that he had to dig in the wetness another day or so. He went down about four and a half feet farther. At last, covered with mud from his hair to his feet, he climbed the ropes to announce that the digging was finished. He went back down to lay up the stone, with his heart light and his hopes high.

Howard Ruede's problems didn't end the day that he found water, but none of them seemed so large after that. Ma wrote that she and Ruthie and

Syd would get along fine in a plastered sod house, so he put off the building of the stone one for awhile in order to tend to his farming. In October, the family was all together again, ready to begin life on their Kansas homestead.

The last of the homestead lands were claimed in a mad race on September 16, 1893, when the Cherokee Strip of Oklahoma was opened to those who wanted it. That day marked the closing of another chapter in America's story.

The Garlands and the Ruedes were just two of the thousands of families who pioneered that great stretch of land from the Rocky Mountains almost to the Mississippi River. Their stories are much like those of most of the others who had the courage to keep on working when it seemed they would never be able to tame the land that Old Mother Nature had held so long. But tame it they did, changing the rough buffalo grass and the waving blue stem to the amber and green of wheat and corn.

The courage and hard work of these sturdy pioneers of the plains helped make America great.